200/1117   ODENTON ELEM   15.38
02-04

IT'S SCIENCE!

Air and Flight

Sally Hewitt

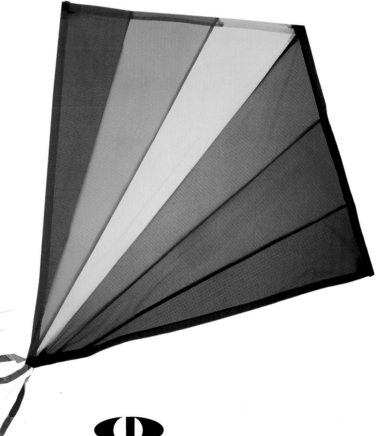

CHILDREN'S PRESS®

A Division of Grolier Publishing

NEW YORK • LONDON • HONG KONG • SYDNEY
DANBURY, CONNECTICUT

Acknowledgments:
Aviation Picture Library/Austin J. Brown pp. 20, 23t, 24b, 25l; Bruce Coleman pp. 7br (Harald Lange),
11t (Hans Reinhard), 11 inset (Colin Varndeel), 19br (Jane Burton), 25r (Guido Cozzi) 26l (Kim Taylor),
26r (Pacific Stock), 27r (Joe McDonald); Robert Harding pp. 16t (Sassoon), 22r; Image Bank pp. 7bl (Terje Rakke),
8b (Anselm Spring), 9, 10b (James Carmichael),17 (David Sharrock), 24t (T. Willett); Images Colour Library p. 8t;
Natural History Photographic Agency p. 19bl (Nigel Dennis); Oxford Scientific Films pp. 11b (Max Gibbs),
22l (Kim Westerskov), 27tl (Alastair Shay), 27bl (Claude Steelman); Steve Shott Cover and title page;
The Stock Market p. 15t. Thanks, too, to our models: Naomi Ramplin, David Watts, Camilla Knipe,
Gemma Suleyman, Conor Pavitt, Shaheen Amirhosseini, James Moller.

Series editor: Rachel Cooke
Designer: Mo Choy
Consultant: Sally Nankivell-Aston
Photography: Ray Moller unless otherwise acknowledged

First published in 1999 by Franklin Watts
96 Leonard Street, London EC2A 4XD

First American edition 2000 by Children's Press
A division of Grolier Publishing
90 Sherman Turnpike, Danbury, CT 06816

Visit Children's Press on the Internet at:
http://publishing.grolier.com

A CIP catalog record for this book is
available from the Library of Congress

ISBN 0-516-21652-X

GROLIER
PUBLISHING

Contents

Air All Around

Air is all around you. It is invisible so you can't see it. You can't smell or taste it either, but you can feel it — just take a deep breath!

 THINK ABOUT IT!

Can you imagine what it would be like if air was a color and you could see it? Do you think it would be more difficult to see the world around you?

 TRY IT OUT!

You can prove that air is all around you by catching it in a bag. Flatten a sandwich bag to push any air out. Hold it out while you whirl around several times. Quickly close the open end and see and feel that the bag is now full of air.

When the air around us moves, we call it wind. You can feel wind blowing on your skin and through your hair.

Wind blows a kite into the air. You have to hold onto the string or it will blow away.

Moving air is a powerful **force**. Wind blows into the sails of a yacht and pushes it along.

The sails of a windmill turn in the wind and work the machinery inside it.

7

What Is Air?

Earth, the planet we live on, is surrounded by a thick layer of air and tiny pieces of dust called the **atmosphere**.

Air is a mixture of different **gases**. The main gases are **oxygen**, **carbon dioxide**, and **nitrogen**. Another is **water vapor** — the water vapor forms the clouds we see in the sky.

💡 THINK ABOUT IT!

Clean air is more healthy for us to breathe into our **lungs**. Where can you go to find clean air to breathe?

Cars and factory chimneys pump out dirty exhaust and smoke into the air.

All living things on Earth need air to live.

There is no air in space, so astronauts — people who travel into space — have to carry a supply of oxygen from Earth's atmosphere so they can breathe.

The moon does not have an atmosphere as Earth does. There is no air there, so nothing can live on the moon.

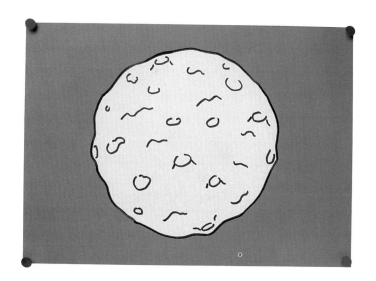

TRY IT OUT!

Have you seen a picture of the surface of the moon? Try drawing your own picture of the moon — imagine what it would be like in a place where there are no living things.

Air for Life

You are breathing air in and out of your lungs all the time, even when you are asleep, because you need oxygen from the air to live.

When you breathe, you take in oxygen and give out carbon dioxide.

👁 LOOK AGAIN

Look again at page 8 to find what else is in the air you breathe.

Even insects breathe. Tiny tubes all along their bodies let air in and out.

Plants need air to live. They take in carbon dioxide and give out oxygen through tiny holes in their leaves. Oxygen from plants helps keep the air good for us to breathe.

Fish breathe in oxygen even though they live underwater and are not surrounded by air. Oxygen from the air dissolves in the water, and fish take it out of the water through their **gills**.

gill

🔆 THINK ABOUT IT!

People cannot stay underwater because, unlike fish, they do not have gills. What do divers take with them so that they can swim underwater for a long time?

11

Full of Air

Air can be mixed into food to make it light. Meringues are made by whisking air into egg whites, adding sugar, and then baking slowly.

 TRY IT OUT!

Break two eggs and pour the whites into a bowl. Whisk until they become white and fluffy. What changes do you notice? Is there more egg white now that you have whisked air into it?

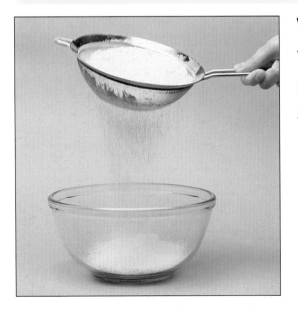

When you make a sponge cake, you sift the flour and "fold" it carefully into the mixture. This puts air into the mixture and helps make a light, spongy cake.

Things that are full of air will usually **float** on water. When you blow into water wings and fill them with air, they help you float when you are learning to swim.

Warm clothes are often full of holes! The holes are not empty — they are full of air. Heat from your body warms up the air trapped in the holes and helps stop you from getting cold.

Air Is Strong

Air pushes against everything — even you, although you can't feel it.

 TRY IT OUT!

Fill a glass to the brim with water. Over a bowl or sink, slide strong cardboard across the rim. Quickly and carefully turn the glass upside down. Let go of the cardboard. It will not fall off, and the water will stay inside the glass — because the air pushing up against the cardboard is stronger than the water pushing down on it.

Tires full of air hold up heavy weights, such as a bus full of people or you on your bicycle. The tires must be made of strong material, too, or they will burst.

A flat tire will give you a very bumpy ride.

 TRY IT OUT!

Blow up a balloon under a pile of toys. Watch how the air in the balloon is strong enough to push the toys over. Now let go of the balloon and watch it fly around as the air escapes.

Hot Air

Hot air spreads out and becomes lighter than cool air. Because it is light, it rises up.

When a hot-air balloon is filled with hot air from a burning flame, it rises up, carrying the heavy basket and its passengers.

As soon as hot air is let out of the balloon, the balloon sinks back down to the ground again.

TRY IT OUT!

Make a mobile of twirling spirals.
1. Draw and cut out circles of colored paper.
2. Draw a spiral in each circle and cut carefully along the lines.
3. Run thread through the center of each spiral.
4. Hang them up above a lamp or radiator. Watch the spirals spin around in the warm, rising air.

Follow the arrows to see how air is always on the move, going around and around.

Warm air rises up and away from the ground and begins to cool down.

The warm ground heats up the air above it.

Cold air moves into the space left by the rising warm air.

The sun shines and heats up the ground.

 THINK ABOUT IT!

Why do you think it is cold at the top of a mountain even though hot air rises?

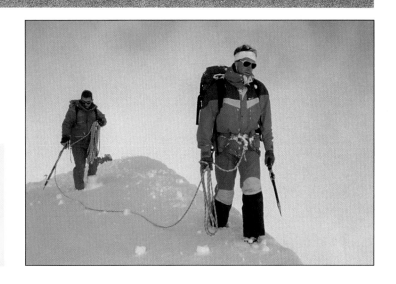

Floating and Falling

When objects like the ones on this page are thrown up into the air, they will all fall down again because of a force called **gravity**. Gravity pulls everything to the ground. But the objects do not all fall in the same way.

These objects fall straight down.

 TRY IT OUT!

Collect some objects. Make sure they are not breakable or sharp. Take them outside, throw them in the air, and watch them come down. Do they float or fall straight down? Record what happens.

These objects float down.

Air slows objects down as they fall because of their shape. A parachute floats down because, as it falls, air collects under it and slows it down.

✋ TRY IT OUT!

You can turn a paper plate into a parachute.

1. Punch out four holes equally spaced around the edge of a paper plate.
2. Cut four lengths of thread and tie one through each hole.
3. Tie a small toy figure to the four loose ends.
4. Throw your parachute up and watch the plate float down to the ground.

Some **seeds** are a good shape for traveling through the air to land away from the plant they came from.

Maple seeds spin through the air on wings.

Fluffy dandelion seeds float on the wind.

19

Flying Shapes

Things that float and drift catch the air as they fall, but they are not a good shape for flying through the air. Things that fly need to move quickly through the air.

 LOOK AGAIN

Look again at pages 18 and 19 to find things that float and drift through the air. What shape are they?

Birds and airplanes are a good shape for flying. They have wings, a pointed nose, and a smooth, **streamlined** shape so that air can slip over them.

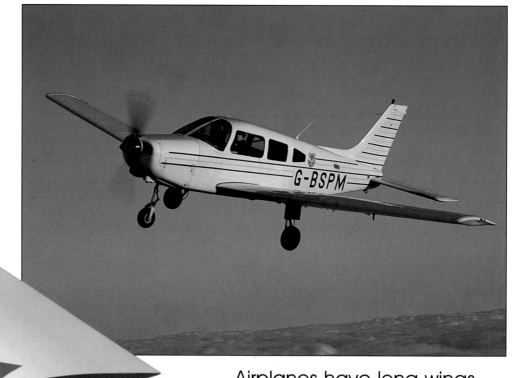

Airplanes have long wings that are curved on the top and flatter underneath. This shape helps lift them into the air and keep them flying.

20

TRY IT OUT!

On a windy day, open an umbrella and run into the wind. What can you feel? Now close the umbrella and point it into the wind as you run. What does it feel like now?

The open umbrella pushes against the air. Air moves easily over the shape of the closed umbrella. Which umbrella makes a better shape for moving fast through the air?

21

Gliding

Gliders don't have **engines** to power them through the air. Sometimes they are towed up into the air by an airplane, or a truck will pull them along until they get up enough speed to take off. They stay up on rising warm air.

 LOOK AGAIN

Look again at page 16 to find why warm air rises.

A light body and long narrow wings help lift the glider up and keep it in the air.

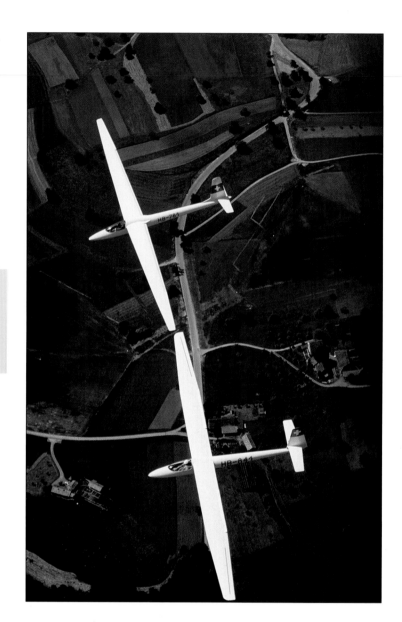

An albatross can glide on rising warm air for a long time without flapping its wings. How is the shape of an albatross the same as the shape of a glider?

22

A hang-glider pilot can run down a hillside to take off into the air. Gliders and hang gliders will gradually go down toward the ground. The pilots look for rising warm air to stay up as long as they can.

 TRY IT OUT!

Make a glider.

1. Fold a sheet of paper in half, then in half again.

2. Copy this shape onto the paper and tear or cut along the line.

3. Unfold the glider shape.

4. Weight the center front with a paper clip and add poster putty if necessary.

5. Hold your glider by the tail and let it go from a height. Test fly it. You can change the shape or the weight a little to help it glide better.

Wings or Rotors?

Airplanes must have wings and engines to fly.

Jet engines power a big passenger airplane. As it speeds along the runway, air rushes over the curved wings and lifts the plane up for takeoff.

Jet engines work by sucking air in at the front and forcing it out through the back.

👁 LOOK AGAIN

Look again at page 15. What happens to an untied balloon when you let go of it and air is pushed out behind it?

Helicopters don't have to speed along a runway to take off. They have long **rotors** with a curved shape. As the rotors spin, air is forced downward, lifting the helicopter straight up into the air.

👁 LOOK AGAIN

Look again at page 20 to see how the shape of a rotor is like the shape of an airplane wing.

A helicopter **hovers**. This means it can hang in the air in one place. It can also move backward, forward, and sideways.

💡 THINK ABOUT IT!

A helicopter is used to rescue people on mountains. Can you think of other jobs a helicopter could be used to do?

Animals in the Air

Birds have wings and a streamlined shape, but instead of having an engine to power them, they use their own energy to flap their wings.

Wings push air downward to lift the bird into the air.

Birds have hollow bones that are light and strong. Their muscles are very powerful for flapping.

🔆 THINK ABOUT IT!

You would need enormous wings to lift you into the air. Think how tired you would get if you had to flap giant wings to fly!

Many insects fly. Insects like flies flap their wings too fast to see. A butterfly flaps its wings more slowly.

A bat has no feathers. It darts through the air on wings of muscles and skin.

A hummingbird flutters its wings very fast in a figure eight. This lets it hover in the air as it drinks nectar from a flower.

 LOOK AGAIN

Look again at page 25 to find an aircraft that hovers.

27

Useful Words

Air Air is a mixture of gases including oxygen, carbon dioxide, nitrogen, and water vapor. We can't see air, but it is all around us. People, animals, and plants need air to live.

Atmosphere The atmosphere is a layer of air, dust, and tiny droplets of water that surrounds Earth. It helps keep Earth warm and protects us from the sun's dangerous rays.

Carbon dioxide Carbon dioxide is one kind of gas in the air. We breathe carbon dioxide out of our lungs.

Engine Machines with moving parts, such as cars and airplanes, have engines. An engine gives them the power they need to work.

Float Boats float on water. Balloons can float in air. They do not sink under the water or down to the ground.

Force A force pushes and pulls an object and makes it move, speed up, slow down, change direction, or change shape.

Gas The air all around us is made up of a mixture of different gases. A gas does not have a shape of its own.

Gills Fish breathe by taking oxygen out of the water with their two gills, one on each side of their head.

Glider Gliders are a kind of flying machine with wings and a streamlined shape but no engine. They stay up on rising warm air.

Gravity Gravity is a kind of natural force. It pulls everything down toward the ground.

Hover Something hovers in the air if it flies but stays in one place.

Jet engines Many airplanes are powered by jet engines. The engine pushes the plane along with air that it sucks in and then forces or jets out again at great speed.

Lungs You have two lungs that are like small bags in your chest. They fill up with air when you breathe in, and empty when you breathe out.

Nitrogen There is more nitrogen in the air than any other gas. It helps living things grow and, when they die, rot.

Oxygen Oxygen is a gas in the air, which you need to live. Your body takes in oxygen when you breathe in.

Rotors Rotors are long blades that spin around, pushing air downward to lift a helicopter off the ground.

Seeds A plant grows from a seed. A seed contains a new plant and a store of food so the plant can begin to grow.

Streamlined Air slips easily over a streamlined shape. Racing cars, airplanes, and birds have streamlined shapes for moving fast through the air.

Water vapor When water is heated it becomes a gas called water vapor. As water vapor cools, it becomes liquid water again.

Index

About This Book

Children are natural scientists. They learn by touching and feeling, noticing, asking questions, and trying things out for themselves. The books in the *It's Science!* series are designed for the way children learn. Familiar objects are used as starting points for further learning. *Air and Flight* starts by showing how air surrounds us and explores air and how things can fly through it.

Each double-page spread introduces a new topic, such as gliding. Information is given, questions asked, and activities suggested that encourage children to make discoveries and develop new ideas for themselves. Look for these panels throughout the book:

TRY IT OUT! indicates a simple activity, using safe materials, that proves or explores a point.

THINK ABOUT IT! indicates a question inspired by the information on the page but that points the reader to areas not covered by the book.

LOOK AGAIN introduces a cross-referencing activity that links themes and facts through the book.

Encourage children not to take the familiar world for granted. Point things out, ask questions, and enjoy making scientific discoveries together.